F•THE irst Ladies

★

OF THE UNITED STATES

Helen Herron Taft

F·THE irst Ladies

★

OF THE UNITED STATES

NICOLA GILLIES

BARNES
&NOBLE
B O O K S
NEW YORK

FOR

GINA GILLIES

Cover photograph: The first lady, Jacqueline Lee Bouvier Kennedy,
sitting on couch, Washington D.C.
© *Mark Shaw/Photo Researchers*

Page 2 photograph: Helen Herron Taft
Courtesy, Corbis-Bettmann

Produced by DoveTail Books

ISBN 0-7607-0542-9

Designed and produced in the United States. Printed in China.

3 5 7 9 8 6 4 2

Foreword

The nonelective role of First Lady has had a decided impact on the course of many presidential terms and on the shape of history. The stories of the First Ladies are as individual as the women who lived them, but they are all of deep human interest and reflect the changing status of women as do few other factors in American history. The First Lady is one of the nation's most visible figures—a daunting role, but most have risen to the challenge with grace and dignity.

To date, there have been forty First Ladies, each different, but all possessing to various degrees the values of loyalty, compassion, strength, courage, and faith. Martha Washington set a strong precedent during her years as First Lady, contributing to the new nation's credibility as a rising power. Abigail Adams presented cogent arguments for women's rights in her correspondence with her husband. Their love story continues to inspire students of American history. Dolley Madison demonstrated the art of being a good hostess, enlivening the White House with her warmth.

With the ascendancy of radio and television, contemporary First Ladies have been thrust into the limelight: the American public is privy to almost every aspect of their lives. Eleanor Roosevelt used her national appeal to champion many important causes, as did several of her successors. When John F. Kennedy was assassinated, the nation grieved along with his widow. Pat Nixon remained loyal to her husband when he was implicated in political wrongdoing. And awareness of drug and alcohol abuse was heightened when Betty Ford shared her battle with addiction. Presented here in brief, then, are the nation's First Ladies, whose history is a microcosm of the history of women in America.

Contents

Martha Dandridge Custis Washington

1731–1802
IST FIRST LADY: 1789–97
4 Children (1st marriage)

ffectionately known as Lady Washington, Martha Dandridge was born in New Kent County, Virginia. Trained to sew, cook, spin, weave, and embroider, she received no formal education, as was typical of her time. Martha married Colonel Daniel Parke Custis, a wealthy planter, when she was eighteen, and they had four children, only two of whom lived past infancy. A year after Custis died, Martha met George Washington, a veteran of the French and Indian War, whom she married in January 1759.

During the Revolutionary War, Martha traveled with her husband and helped nurse the wounded soldiers. When separated from Washington, she made clothing and gathered supplies for the soldiers, while maintaining the family's large plantation at Mount Vernon.

In 1789 the first Electoral College elected Washington president, and Martha took upon herself the responsibilities that came with her husband's new position, wholeheartedly supporting Washington during both of his terms. She was a dignified hostess whose graciousness set a precedent for future First Ladies. Entertaining was a formal affair that illustrated the new republic's intention of being regarded as an equal among the older European governments. Martha's warm personality helped make her guests feel at ease.

Overjoyed when Washington announced that he would not seek a third term as president, Martha returned to Mount Vernon to resume her life as an "old fashioned Virginia housekeeper." When Washington died in December 1799, she closed up their bedroom and took a smaller room for herself. In the belief that she had shared enough of her private life with the American public, she carefully burned nearly all of the letters that Washington had written her during their marriage. Martha died in 1802 and was buried beside Washington at Mount Vernon, which would become a national shrine.

Abigail Smith Adams

1744—1818
2ND FIRST LADY: 1797—1801
5 Children

orn in Weymouth, Massachusetts, the daughter of a minister, Abigail Smith suffered from poor health in childhood. She was a voracious reader; under the tutelage of her father, she was educated by the books in their library. A woman of her own mind, Abigail married the young lawyer John Adams in 1764 against her family's wishes after a three year courtship. The mutual devotion of the young couple soon dispelled any doubts that Abigail's parents had felt.

Interested in politics, Abigail shared her husband's views on Colonial America's relationship with Great Britain. Her sharp business sense enabled her to keep the family financially secure while Adams was in the field against the British during the Revolutionary War. Determined to do her share for the war effort, Abigail opened her home in Braintree (now Quincy), Massachusetts, to the wounded and to refugees. The correspondence between John Adams and his wife during their many separations would form a valuable contribution to the historical record.

After eight years of service as Washington's vice-president, Adams was elected president in 1797, and the couple moved into the nearly completed Presidents' House in Washington, D.C. During her years as First Lady, Abigail continued the social gatherings initiated by Martha Washington. She was responsible for organizing the first full-dress reception on New Year's Day in 1801. A woman ahead of her time, Abigail believed that slavery should be abolished and wrote to her husband declaring that slaves have "as good a right to freedom as we have." She was also a strong advocate of women's rights and encouraged Adams to "remember the ladies and be more generous than your ancestors."

In 1801 the couple returned to their Massachusetts farm. Seven years after Abigail's death in 1818, her son, John Quincy Adams, was elected to the highest office, making her the first woman to be both wife and mother of a United States president.

Dolley Payne Todd Madison

1768–1849
3RD FIRST LADY: 1809–17
2 Children (1st marriage)

Dolley Payne spent the first fifteen years of her life in Scotchtown, Virginia, before moving in 1783 to Philadelphia. There she met and married her first husband, John Todd, who was a Quaker lawyer. Tragically, during the yellow fever epidemic of 1793, she lost both her husband and one of their two beloved sons. A handsome and engaging woman, Dolley overcame her grief with great fortitude. She met James Madison, then a member of the House of Representatives, in 1794, and the two were married later that year.

The couple moved to Montpelier, the Madison homestead in Virginia, where they frequently visited with their neighbor Thomas Jefferson at Monticello. When Jefferson was elected president in 1800, Madison became his secretary of state, and Dolley helped arrange the widowed Jefferson's social engagements and entertain guests to the President's House.

The first inaugural ball was held in Washington, D.C., when Madison assumed the presidency in 1809. Dolley soon became known as an engaging hostess who planned weekly state dinners and "dove parties" for the cabinet wives. When the British set fire to Washington, D.C., during the War of 1812, it was the resourceful Dolley Madison who secured most of the possessions of the presidential mansion.

The Madisons returned to Washington for a second term, after which they retired to Montpelier. After Madison's death in 1836, Congress honored Dolley with a seat in the visitor's gallery of the House of Representatives. At her home on Lafayette Square, she collected her husband's papers on the Constitution, of which he was a principal architect. Congress acquired these papers for posterity on Dolley's eightieth birthday. She died on July 12, 1849, and was buried beside Madison. Her funeral was attended by past and present government officials who honored the true patriotism of this extraordinary First Lady.

Elizabeth Kortright Monroe

1768–1830
4TH FIRST LADY: 1817–25
3 Children

As a representative from Virginia to the Continental Congress, James Monroe was captivated when he met seventeen-year-old Elizabeth Kortright in New York City, her birthplace, in 1785. They married that same year and moved to Virginia. Admired in France as "la belle Américaine," Elizabeth accompanied her husband abroad when he became minister to France; there she was instrumental in freeing the imprisoned wife of the Marquis de Lafayette, who had contributed so generously to the cause of freedom for the American colonies.

Frequent illness limited Elizabeth's attendance at official functions, but she was regarded as a gracious and regal hostess. The President's House became known as the White House when she had the exterior painted a gleaming white, and she furnished the mansion with fashionable French imports. She favored a formal, European atmosphere at the White House.

Distant in manner, and for the most part removed from the political scene, Elizabeth was regarded by many as a snob and formed few close relationships. However, her social acumen during her husband's two terms set a strong precedent for future First Ladies. After Monroe's retirement in 1825, the couple returned to Oak Hill, Virginia, where Elizabeth died in 1830.

Louisa Catherine Johnson Adams

1775–1852
5TH FIRST LADY: 1825–29
4 Children

The only first lady to be born abroad (in London, England), Louisa Catherine Johnson, the daughter of a British citizen and an American diplomat, met John Quincy Adams in 1794, when he came to England as minister to the Netherlands. Three years later, Louisa and the son of former president John Adams were married. They lived in Berlin, Germany, until 1801, when they returned to the United States, and the twenty-six-year-old Louisa saw her father's and husband's homeland for the first time. In fact, she had been more comfortable with her role at the Prussian court than she was during her first few years in the New England farming communities of Braintree (later Quincy), Massachusetts.

In 1809 Adams returned to Europe as minister to Russia with his by now cosmopolitan wife, who traveled with her husband throughout the course of his diplomatic career. He was sent from Russia to Belgium and then to London in 1814. Louisa embarked that winter on a forty-day journey across Europe, traveling by coach to join her husband. The trip was a dangerous one for a single woman, and Louisa and her youngest son also braved unusually harsh weather. They arrived safely in England, where they spent the next two years.

Louisa Catherine Johnson Adams

Adams's accomplishments abroad led to his appointment as secretary of state by President James Monroe in 1817. The Adams drawing room soon became a gathering place for diplomats and other public figures. Their distinguished guests were entertained by Louisa's justly renowned skill in playing the harp and by her theater parties.

In 1824 Adams was elected president in a bitter contest that pitted him against Southerners Henry Clay, Andrew Jackson, and William H. Crawford. His wife's status as a former foreign national was used against him, a factor that may have contributed to the depression that had affected Louisa since the death of their year-old daughter in Russia in 1812.

Despite suffering from increasing ill health, Louisa resolved to continue her Tuesday-evening "at homes" when she took up residence in the White House. During her years as First Lady, she hosted a reception honoring the sixty-eighth birthday of the Marquis de Lafayette and organized the first wedding ceremony of a president's son to take place in the White House. Humility was one of her strengths: when she wrote her life story (which she dedicated to her children), she modestly entitled it *Adventures of a Nobody*.

Intelligent, talented, gracious, and serene, Louisa supported her husband both emotionally and politically during his term as president and the seventeen years that he served in the House of Representatives. In 1847 they celebrated their fiftieth wedding anniversary. A year later, Adams collapsed suddenly and died of a stroke in the Speaker's Room of the Capitol. Louisa survived him by only four years. She was buried beside her husband at the family church in Quincy.

Anna Symmes Harrison

1775–1864
6TH FIRST LADY: Mar. 4–
   Apr. 4, 1841
10 Children

Born in Morristown, New Jersey, Anna Symmes accompanied her father and stepmother to North Bend, Ohio, in 1794. There she met William Henry Harrison, then a captain at Fort Washington, Ohio. An educated and headstrong woman, Anna disregarded her father's objections and eloped with Harrison in November 1795. In 1800 Harrison resigned from the army and became governor of the Indiana territory.

During the War of 1812, Anna moved back to her father's home, and in 1814 Harrison and Anna purchased a farm near North Bend. When Harrison won the presidential election of 1840, Anna's dreams of a quiet retirement vanished. Ill and unable to travel with her husband to Washington in 1841, she sent her daughter-in-law, Jane Irwin Harrison, to represent her. The sixty-five-year-old Anna remained at home, awaiting news of the inaugural festivities. Instead, she learned that her husband had contracted pneumonia during his inauguration. On April 4, 1841, before she could reach him, Harrison became the first president to die in office. In 1858 their home in North Bend burned, and Anna moved to another house nearby. She died there in 1864, twenty-five years before her grandson, Benjamin Harrison, was sworn in as the twenty-third president.

Letitia Christian Tyler

1790–1842

7TH FIRST LADY: Apr. 4, 1841–
   Sept. 10, 1842

8 Children

L etitia Christian was the daughter of a wealthy planter of New Kent County, Virginia. She was courted by John Tyler for five years before her father consented to their marriage in 1813. Letitia's skills at managing a large household allowed Tyler to pursue his political career.

Tyler was chosen as Harrison's running mate on the Whig ticket in the 1840 campaign. He was sworn in as president in April 1841, following Harrison's untimely death. The Tylers moved into the White House, which had been bereft of a First Lady since 1829. Unfortunately, Letitia's health broke down. Partially paralyzed and confined to a wheelchair, she was unable to share her husband's busy social life, although she continued to manage the household. She lived in seclusion at the White House, making her only public appearance at the wedding of her daughter Elizabeth in 1842.

In September 1842, Letitia became the first wife of a president to die during his term of office. The White House was draped in black in remembrance of this gentle woman, and she was buried in Virginia. After Letitia's death, Tyler's presidency began to erode due to conflicts within his own party: he narrowly avoided impeachment in January 1843. In 1844 Tyler married again, becoming the first president to marry while in office.

Julia Gardiner Tyler

1820–89
8TH FIRST LADY: Jun. 26, 1844–
   Mar. 5, 1845
7 Children

Born in Long Island, New York, Julia Gardiner arrived in Washington, D.C., in 1843. There she was introduced to the widowed President Tyler by her father, a former state senator. Widely admired for her beauty (she was called the "Rose of Long Island"), Julia refused Tyler's initial proposals of marriage because of their thirty-year age difference. The sudden death of her father helped alleviate her doubts, and on June 26, 1844, Julia was secretly married to Tyler.

A vibrant hostess, Julia restored the White House to its former status as a center of social activity. She ignored the criticism provoked by her marriage and was his loyal supporter throughout their marriage. She shared Tyler's elation over the admission of the Republic of Texas to the Union and his dismay at being nicknamed the "Veto President" due to partisan politics.

Retiring from public life in 1845, the couple moved to Sherwood Forest, Tyler's estate in Richmond, Virginia, where they raised seven children of their own in addition to those from Tyler's previous marriage. After his death in 1862, Julia devoted herself to volunteer work for the Confederacy. She spent the years before her death in 1889 defending John Tyler's memory and political record and was buried beside him at Sherwood Forest.

Sarah Childress Polk

1803–91

9TH FIRST LADY: 1845–49

A devout Presbyterian, Sarah Childress was born in Murfreesboro, Tennessee, to a wealthy merchant's family. Educated at the Moravian "female academy" at Salem, North Carolina, she married politician James Knox Polk on January 1, 1824, shortly before he was elected to Congress. During Polk's years in Congress (1825–39), Sarah helped her husband write speeches and served as his unofficial secretary.

When Polk won the presidential election of 1844, Sarah's strong political acumen enabled her to become his official confidential secretary. The new First Lady's religious beliefs soon put an end to many of the former social activities at the White House. Dancing, drinking, card-playing, and Sunday visits were replaced by twice-weekly receptions where no refreshments were served.

In March 1849, the couple retired to their home in Nashville, Tennessee, where Polk died three months later. His last words were a declaration of his love for his wife. Sarah turned their home into a shrine, preserving all of Polk's papers and opening her doors to his admirers. She went out only to attend church services. "Polk Place" became a place of pilgrimage for those who had esteemed the populist president. Sarah Childress Polk died in 1891 and was buried beside her husband.

Margaret Smith Taylor

1788–1852
10TH FIRST LADY: Mar. 5,
  1849–July 9, 1850
6 Children

Margaret Smith moved from her native Calvert County, Maryland, to live with her married sister in Kentucky after their father's death. Zachary Taylor, on leave from the army, had returned to his Kentucky homestead in 1809. Taylor and Margaret met later that year and were married in 1810.

A devoted wife and mother, Margaret followed her husband from one frontier outpost to another, risking the dangers of the Indian Wars in order to keep her family together. Taylor distinguished himself as a major general in the Army's western division, and his heroic victory over Santa Anna's army at Buena Vista, Mexico, ensured him the Whig candidacy in the presidential election of 1848. Taylor accepted the nomination despite his own misgivings and Margaret's belief that his nomination "was a plot to deprive her of his society and shorten his life."

Margaret was in her sixties when she moved into the White House in 1849. Poor health kept her confined to her rooms, from which she emerged only for small family dinners and to attend church services. Her worst fears were realized on July 9, 1850, when Taylor died suddenly of cholera. Distraught at the loss of her husband, Margaret survived him by only two years. They were both buried in the family plot near Louisville, Kentucky.

Abigail Powers Fillmore

1798–1853
11TH FIRST LADY: July 10,
  1850–Mar. 3, 1853
2 Children

A bigail Powers, born in Stillwater, New York, was a teacher at the age of sixteen. She met Millard Fillmore, then nineteen, when he arrived at her classroom in New Hope, New York, 1816. Encouraged by her, Fillmore applied himself to his studies and eventually became a lawyer. He settled in East Aurora, New York, and married Abigail in 1826. Despite her newly married status, Abigail continued to teach until the birth of her son in 1828.

In 1830 the Fillmore family moved to Buffalo, New York, and by 1848 Fillmore had risen from a congressman in the Whig party to comptroller of New York to vice-president in Zachary Taylor's administration. Taylor's untimely death in 1850 resulted in Fillmore's assumption of the presidency. Abigail, increasingly frail, became the eleventh First Lady.

Apprehensive about her husband's health in the wake of Taylor's fatal attack of cholera, she had running water, a modern bathroom, and a modern iron range for cooking installed in the White House. Her love of books inspired her to start a library, a new addition to the executive mansion. Despite her own failing health, Abigail continued to host Tuesday receptions and Friday social gatherings during her husband's term. She died only weeks after Franklin Pierce replaced Fillmore as president in 1853.

Jane Means Appleton Pierce

1806–63
12TH FIRST LADY: 1853–57
3 Children

The wife of the youngest president to that date spent most of her White House years in seclusion. Jane Appleton met Franklin Pierce in 1828 and married him six years later, when he was a member of the House of Representatives. Two years later, in 1836, Pierce was elected to the Senate.

In order to spend more time with his wife, Pierce resigned from the Senate in 1842 and remained at home until 1846, when he enlisted to fight in the Mexican War. It was against Jane's wishes that Pierce accepted the nomination for the presidency in 1852. The earlier loss of two of her three sons bacame too much for her to bear when she suffered the loss of her third son two months before Pierce's inauguration.

These bereavements overshadowed her years as First Lady. Jane spent most of her first two years in the White House confined to her bedroom. On January 1, 1855, she emerged to attend a New Year's party, but could not participate in the mood of the celebration. Although she began attending more and more functions with her husband, her manner was always subdued and detached. Pierce hoped that Jane would be restored to her former self when they left the White House in 1856, but her condition only worsened during their long trip abroad and she died on December 2, 1863.

Mary Todd Lincoln

1818–82

4 Children

13TH FIRST LADY: Mar. 4,
1861–Apr. 15, 1865

A well-educated woman, Mary Todd was born in Lexington, Kentucky, to a banking family. She met Abraham Lincoln, then a lawyer and member of the state legislature, in 1839, when she went to live with her sister in Springfield, Illinois. Their tumultuous courtship, marked by one canceled wedding date, lasted until 1842, when they were finally married.

In 1860 Lincoln was nominated for president under the slogan "The Union Must and Shall Be Preserved." His victory at the polls had been prophesied by Mary years earlier. While many regard Lincoln as the nation's greatest president, opinions concerning his wife's role as First Lady vary. She arrived at the White House when opposition between the North and the South was rapidly increasing, and the Southern belles who greeted her were scornful of her. Determined never to be outshone (or outdressed) again, Mary became obsessed with outfitting herself in outlandishly expensive clothing.

Long subject to severe headaches and violent mood swings (Lincoln called them Mary's "nervous spells"), she became increasingly worse at the White House. Her irrational behavior led some observers to accuse her of spying for the Confederacy. His wife's mental illness was an added burden to Lincoln during the years of the Civil War that raged across the nation.

Shortly after Lincoln was re-elected, he was assassinated by John Wilkes Booth at Ford's Theater. Overcome with grief, Mary was unable to attend the funeral. The political enemies she had made during her years as First Lady and the fears of poverty that plagued her led her to flee abroad with her son Tad. Six years later, in 1871, they returned to the United States. When Tad died suddenly, Mary broke down completely. Her son Robert institutionalized her in 1875. Released several months later, blind and paralyzed, she died on July 16, 1882. Contemporary evidence suggests that she may have suffered from a stroke.

Eliza McCardle Johnson

1810–76
14TH FIRST LADY: Apr. 15,
  1865–Mar. 3, 1869
5 Children

A native of Leesburg, Tennessee, Eliza McCardle became a teacher in Greensville, Tennessee, where she met Andrew Johnson, then a tailor. The couple married in 1827, and Eliza taught Johnson to read and write. His business thrived, and his shop became a political meeting place for local craftsmen.

Johnson became an alderman on Greenville's town council in 1828 and was then elected mayor. He served two terms in the Tennessee house of representatives and one in the state senate before he was elected to Congress. An adamant supporter of her husband's politics, Eliza did not waver even when his antisecession views endangered their family during the Civil War years.

After serving as Lincoln's second vice-president for only six weeks, Johnson was sworn in as president on April 15, 1865, after Lincoln's assassination. Eliza was in poor health for most of her husband's term, but she continued to encourage him with her strength of character and good-natured disposition. A divided Congress impeached Johnson, who was acquitted by one vote in 1868, but he was not truly exonerated until 1875, when he was elected to the Senate. He died later that summer, followed a few months later by Eliza, at peace in knowing that her husband's name had been restored. They are buried in Greensville.

Julia Boggs Dent Grant

1826–1902
15TH FIRST LADY: 1869–77
4 Children

J ulia Boggs Dent met Ulysses S. Grant when he was stationed in St. Louis with the Fourth Infantry Regiment. The two were engaged in 1844, but were not married until August 22, 1848, when the Mexican War ended. Julia happily accepted the arduous life of a military wife, following her husband from post to post.

General Grant's victory over Robert E. Lee, who surrendered at Appomattox Court House, Virginia, in 1865, resulted in his nomination and election to the presidency — years that Julia would refer to later as "the happiest period of my life." Julia transformed the White House into an elegant and extravagant tribute to the Gilded Age. Under her direction, parties became lavish affairs, with dinners of twenty to thirty courses. Her personal popularity remained constant despite the scandals that were rampant during her husband's second term.

After Grant's presidency ended, the couple embarked on a journey around the world before retiring to their home in Mt. McGregor, New York, where bad business decisions resulted in bankruptcy. In order to provide for Julia, Grant worked feverishly to complete his memoirs of the Civil War during his final illness in 1885. He finished only days before he died of cancer. In 1902 Julia was buried with him in New York City.

Lucy Ware Webb Hayes

1831–89
16TH FIRST LADY: 1877–81
8 Children

Educated at Wesleyan Female College in Cincinnati, Ohio, Lucy Webb was the first wife of a president to possess a college degree. Born in Chillicothe, Ohio, she married Rutherford Birchard Hayes, a young lawyer, on December 30, 1852.

An active opponent of slavery, Lucy nursed wounded Union soldiers during the Civil War, earning the affectionate name of "Mother Lucy." When Hayes was elected to the executive office in 1876, his wife brought her religious convictions with her, organizing morning prayer services and evening hymns. She received the nickname "Lemonade Lucy" when she banned alcoholic beverages from the White House, but her receptions were widely praised for their unpretentious and relaxed atmosphere. Deeply in love, Lucy and Hayes renewed their wedding vows at the White House on their twenty-fifth anniversary, in 1877. Admired for her intelligence and cheerful nature, Lucy was praised by one of her guests as being representative of "the new woman era."

Hayes did not run for a second term, and the couple retired to Spiegel Grove, their home near Fremont, Ohio, in 1881. Hayes abandoned politics for humanitarian pursuits. Lucy remained active in child welfare, prison reform, and missionary work until her death in 1889. She is buried at her home in Fremont.

Lucretia Rudolph Garfield

1832–1918
17TH FIRST LADY: Mar. 4–
   Sept. 19, 1881
7 Children
"Crete"

Lucretia Rudolph was born in Ohio to a farming family. During her years at Hiram College, she met James Abram Garfield, but the two went their separate ways after graduation. Garfield returned to teach at Hiram College in 1856 and became college president a year later. They married in 1858.

Garfield was elected to the House of Representatives in 1863, and Lucretia (he called her "Crete") spent the next seventeen years dividing her time between their Ohio and Washington homes. She was primarily responsible for managing the Ohio household, a task she had assumed when Garfield was in the Civil War. He was elected president in 1880, and two months after his inauguration, Lucretia contracted malaria and was sent to a seaside resort in New Jersey to recover. Garfield returned to Washington, D.C., where he was shot by Charles Guiteau on July 2, 1881.

Still frail herself, Lucretia returned to nurse her husband through the summer, while doctors attempted unsuccessfully to find the hidden bullet. Garfield finally succumbed to his wound in September 1881. His assassin was tried and hanged the following year. In an outpouring of support, friends of the couple raised money that would support his widow until her death on March 14, 1918. She spent her last years preserving the records of her husband's career.

Frances Folsom Cleveland

1864–1947
18TH AND 20TH FIRST LADY:
Jun. 2, 1886–1889, 1893–97
5 Children
"Frank"

B orn in Buffalo, New York, Frances Folsom captured the heart of America when she married Grover Cleveland in the first White House wedding of a president. Cleveland and Frances's father were law partners. Cleveland helped plan Frances's education and began courting her when she entered Wells College. His own career took him from the governorship of New York to the presidency in 1884.

Frances visited the White House with her mother in mid-1885, a few months after Cleveland had been inaugurated. Their courtship became a full-fledged romance, and, despite their twenty-seven-year age difference, the two were married on June 2, 1886. The historical event took place in the Blue Room.

As First Lady, Frances held twice-weekly receptions and won the affection of her guests, who were impressed with her unaffected personality. During Cleveland's second term, when the president struggled with financial and social disorder, the couple spent most of their time at their farm near Washington and their house in the suburbs. In 1897 they moved to Princeton, New Jersey, where Cleveland died at their home, "Westland," in 1908. Five years later, Frances remarried. In keeping with custom, she was referred to as Mrs. Cleveland until her death in 1947.

Caroline Lavinia Scott Harrison

1832–92
19TH FIRST LADY: 1889–
   Oct. 25, 1892
2 Children

Caroline Scott met Benjamin Harrison, the grandson of William Henry Harrison, while he was a student at Miami University, Oxford, Ohio. They married in 1853 and moved to Indianapolis, where Harrison set up his law practice. During the Civil War, Caroline helped nurse wounded Union soldiers. She spent most of her time in Indianapolis during Harrison's years in the Senate (1881–87).

Harrison was elected president in 1888. A year later, Caroline was honored by being named first president-general of the Daughters of the American Revolution. During her years as First Lady, she modernized the interior of the White House. She installed the first electric lights and doorbells in 1891. Caroline was also responsible for setting up the first White House Christmas tree in the Oval Room, which became a tradition, and established the collection of china associated with the Executive Mansion.

Caroline died of tuberculosis in the White House on October 25, 1892. Services were held in the East Room of the mansion, and she was buried from her own First Presbyterian Church in Indianapolis. Devastated by the loss of his wife, Harrison lost the election of 1892 to Grover Cleveland and returned to Indiana.

Ida Saxton McKinley

1847–1907
21ST FIRST LADY: Mar. 4,
   1897–Sept. 14, 1901
2 Children

The daughter of an advocate for women's rights, Ida Saxton was educated at both a local Canton, Ohio, school and a finishing school, and sent to Europe for the Grand Tour by her father. She then worked in her father's bank as a cashier. William McKinley, who had a local law practice, was captivated by Ida: the two fell in love and married in 1871.

Ida left her job at the bank to become a full-time wife and mother, but she soon became seriously ill with phlebitis and epilepsy. Both her children died in infancy and by 1876 Ida was an invalid who would be confined to a chair for the rest of her life. When McKinley became president in 1897, Ida was determined to do her duty as First Lady despite her poor health.

Seated in a blue velvet chair with a bouquet of flowers in her hands, Ida graciously greeted guests at the White House. In order to enable McKinley to monitor his wife's seizures, tradition was abandoned, and Ida was seated beside her husband at state dinners. The press and her guests were considerate and little was revealed to the public about her condition, referred to privately as "fainting spells." Her husband's assassination in 1901 was a shattering blow. She visited his grave almost daily until her death in 1907, when she was buried beside McKinley and their daughters.

Edith Kermit Carow Roosevelt

1861–1948
22ND FIRST LADY: Sept. 14,
   1901–Mar. 3, 1909
5 Children

Although Edith Carow and Theodore Roosevelt had grown up with each other in New York City, they did not become romantically involved until after the death of Roosevelt's first wife, Alice Hathaway Lee. Edith married the twenty-eight-year-old Roosevelt in London in December 1886 and moved into a house on Sagamore Hill, Oyster Bay, Long Island.

When President McKinley was killed by an assassin in 1901, Vice-President Roosevelt became the youngest president to that date. Edith assumed the role of First Lady with a strong sense of decorum. She did not invite guests back to the White House if they broke her moral and social rules. At her instigation, the first social secretary was employed, allowing her to devote more time to her family. During Edith's years as First Lady, the White House was enlarged and modernized, and a picture gallery of all the First Ladies was created in the ground-floor corridor.

The Roosevelts retired to Sagamore Hill in 1909. Roosevelt died there ten years later. Edith spent her remaining years traveling abroad, but returned frequently to Sagamore Hill. She continued her work on behalf of Christ Church at Oyster Bay and the Needlework Guild, which provided clothing for the poor, until her death in 1948.

Helen Herron Taft

1861–1943
23RD FIRST LADY: 1909–13

3 Children
"Nellie"

Helen Herron was the daughter of a wealthy lawyer of Cincinnati, Ohio. An accomplished pianist, she was educated in a private school. At the age of seventeen, she visited the White House with her parents, who were friends of President and Mrs. Rutherford Hayes. Helen was so impressed that she declared she would be First Lady one day.

Intelligent and politically astute, Helen eventually organized her own "literary salon" for weekly discussions of books, music, and politics. When she was eighteen, she met William Howard Taft, then a young lawyer, at a sledding party; he was captivated by her intelligence. Taft became a regular participant in her salons, and in 1886 the two were married. Helen had great aspirations for her husband and contributed substantially to his political career while remaining actively involved with her community. She helped to establish the Cincinnati Symphony Orchestra before traveling to the Philippines in 1900, when Taft was appointed governor there.

Taft was offered an appointment to the Supreme Court by President Theodore Roosevelt, but Helen urged him to run for president in the election of 1908. Although he preferred the Supreme Court to the Executive Office, he followed his wife's advice, and in 1909 the couple moved into the White House, Helen riding there with her husband, which was unprecedented. She suffered a stroke two months after the inauguration, but quickly recovered to become an engaging and active hostess.

Her years as First Lady are memorialized by the Japanese Cherry trees that she had planted around the Tidal Basin. She was also responsible for erecting a stand in Potomac Park for concerts. Inside the White House, Helen furnished the Oval Office with Oriental furniture reminiscent of her years in the East. Widowed in 1930, she remained in the capital and published her memoirs, *Recollections of Full Years,* before her death in 1943.

Ellen Louise Axson Wilson

1860–1914
24TH FIRST LADY: 1913–
   Aug. 6, 1914
3 Children

Born in Savannah, Georgia, the daughter of a Presbyterian minister, Ellen Axson grew up in Rome, Georgia. She was a talented artist and studied painting at the Art Students' League of New York and also attended Georgia's Shorter College. Ellen met Thomas Woodrow Wilson, a young lawyer, when he was visiting in Rome in 1883, and the two married in 1885. During their marriage, they exchanged 1,400 love letters.

Wilson was nominated for president in 1912, and the couple moved into the White House the following spring. Ellen immediately installed a studio with a skylight: she sold or donated many of her paintings to various charities. Appalled by conditions in the capital's slums, she urged Congress to draft housing legislation and donated time and money to improving living conditions for the poor. Described as "the angel in the White House," she kept social gatherings simple: her dislike of lavish formal parties led to the Wilsons' decision not to have an Inaugural Ball.

Ellen fell gravely ill with Bright's disease in the spring of 1914, and the seriousness of her condition spurred Congress to pass the housing legislation she had inspired. She died on August 6, 1914, and the grieving Wilson accompanied her body to her family burial place in Rome, Georgia.

Edith Bolling Galt Wilson

1872–1961
25TH FIRST LADY:
Dec. 18, 1915–Mar. 4, 1921

Described as "perhaps the most controversial First Lady," Edith Bolling, of Wytheville, Virginia, was the seventh of eleven children. She studied music at Martha Washington College and also attended a small college in Richmond. In 1896 she married Norman Galt, who died suddenly in 1908.

The widowed President Wilson met Edith in Washington and was captivated by her intelligence and beauty. He married her on December 18, 1915. While some were outraged at a new First Lady so soon after Ellen Wilson's death the previous year, others described Edith as a "blessing and delight to President Wilson." Social events at the White House were ruled out during Wilson's second term, when the United States joined World War I (April 1917). Edith learned the codes for communicating with emissaries abroad and was active in Red Cross volunteer work. When Wilson suffered two strokes late in his second term, she became the official acting president, assuming unprecedented responsibility — a period she described in *My Memoir,* published in 1939.

Widowed in 1924, Edith spent her remaining years honoring her husband's accomplishments. She served as director of the Woodrow Wilson Foundation, and her home was left to the National Trust for Historic Preservation after her death in 1961.

Florence Kling DeWolfe Harding

1860–1924

26TH FIRST LADY: Mar. 4,
   1921–Aug. 2, 1923

1 Child (1st marriage)

Florence Kling was born in Marion, Ohio, the daughter of successful businessman Amos Kling. A strong-willed woman, she eloped at nineteen with a neighbor, Henry DeWolfe, who abandoned her and their son shortly after their marriage. Florence returned to Marion and eventually filed for divorce — a bold decision in the late 1800s. She supported herself and her son by giving piano lessons, having attended the Cincinnati Conservatory of Music before her marriage.

Florence met William Harding shortly after he moved to Marion and bought the local newspaper, *The Daily Star*. Florence ignored her father's advice again and married Harding in 1891. Although her father adopted her son, he would not speak to her for seven years. When Harding fell ill, she directed the *Star's* circulation department, and the paper prospered. She remained there for fourteen years. Despite evidence of Harding's infidelity, Florence supported his rise through Ohio politics to the U.S. Senate and encouraged him to run for president in 1920.

Florence's years as First Lady began on March 4, 1921, when she embarked on a full schedule of receptions and gatherings. Harding's lack of interest in his presidential responsibilities was outdistanced by her enthusiasm. Despite the fact that she suffered from a kidney ailment, she met regularly with Harding's cabinet officials and took an active part in policymaking. Always cheerful and smartly dressed, she visited hospitals and held White House garden parties for veterans.

The rumors of corruption that shadowed Harding's administration prompted the couple to embark on a cross-country "Voyage of Understanding" by rail. They set out in June 1923, but the trip was cut short in California, where Harding died suddenly in August. Shaken by the financial scandals that were revealed shortly afterward, Florence burned virtually all of his papers. She died in Marion only fifteen months later.

Grace Anna Goodhue Coolidge

1879–1957
27TH FIRST LADY: Aug. 3,
    1923–Mar. 3, 1929
2 Children

G race Goodhue, born in Burlington, Vermont, graduated from the University of Vermont in 1902 and moved to Northampton, Massachusetts. There she taught at the Clarke School for the Deaf until her marriage to Calvin Coolidge.

Coolidge's political career was well underway when they married and in 1921 he became Warren Harding's vice-president. In 1923 Harding's sudden death made him president.

Grace's social gatherings were praised for their dignity and warmth. When the roof of the White House was declared unsafe in 1927, she made plans for its renovation. She also created the "Sky Parlor" sun-room, and it was largely due to her influence that Congress passed legislation allowing the acceptance of appropriate gifts for the White House. Not even the grief of her younger son's death at the age of sixteen prevented her from carrying out her duties with tact and cordiality. She received a gold medal from the National Institute of Social Sciences for her "fine personal influence exerted as First Lady," and in 1931 she was honored as one of the nation's twelve greatest living women.

In 1929 the Coolidges retired to Northampton, where Calvin Coolidge died in 1933. Grace served as a trustee for the Clarke School for the Deaf until her death in 1957.

Lou Henry Hoover

1874–1944
28TH FIRST LADY: 1929–33
2 Children

Linguist, scholar, outdoorswoman, and geologist, Lou Henry, of Waterloo, Iowa, was a talented and versatile woman. She met Herbert Hoover at California's Stanford University and married him on February 10, 1899.

The couple moved to China, where Hoover had been appointed a mining consultant to the imperial government. During the Boxer Rebellion of 1898–01, Lou nursed the wounded. The young couple translated the sixteenth-century folio *De Re Metallica* from Latin to English and eventually traveled all over the world as Hoover's career prospered. They moved into the White House in 1929, and Lou began research for a history of its furnishings. She privately commissioned reproductions of Monroe furnishings for the Red Room and restored Lincoln's study for Hoover's use. As the economy worsened during the Great Depression, the Hoovers used their own money to fund gatherings at the White House.

Hoover's term ended in 1933, and the couple retired to their home in Palo Alto, California, where they continued to support various charities. Lou worked with the Salvation Army and served as president of the national organization of Girl Scouts before her death in 1944. The widowed Hoover described her as "a symbol of everything wholesome in American life."

Anna Eleanor Roosevelt Roosevelt

1884–1962

29TH FIRST LADY: Mar. 4,
1933–Apr. 12, 1945

6 Children

O rphaned at the age of ten, Eleanor Roosevelt, the daughter of Anna Hall and Elliot Roosevelt, went to live with her maternal grandmother and was educated in England. She returned to New York City, her birthplace, for her debut and renewed her friendship with Franklin Delano Roosevelt, a distant cousin. The two became engaged and, despite the initial reservations of Franklin's strong-willed mother, Sara Delano Roosevelt, they were married in 1905. President Theodore Roosevelt, Eleanor's uncle, gave the bride away.

When her husband was stricken with polio while serving as a New York senator in 1921, Eleanor became his invaluable assistant. During these years, she worked with New York State's Democratic Committee, sharing his interest in politics. Elected governor of New York in 1928, he went on to the presidency in 1933, destined to remain in office longer than anyone else in American history. Eleanor overcame the shyness that plagued her as a young woman to develop her own strong political career in addition to supporting her husband's.

In the White House, Eleanor broke with precedent and held press conferences of her own, as well as writing a daily syndicated newspaper column called "My Day." Sensitive to the needs of the underprivileged, she helped establish the National Youth Administration, won equal pay for women in industry under the National Recovery Administration, and encouraged desegregation of public facilities. When African-American contralto Marian Anderson was banned from singing at Constitution Hall by the Daughters of the American Revolution, Eleanor resigned from the organization and arranged for the concert to be held at the Lincoln Memorial.

As First Lady, Eleanor presided over White House gatherings for twelve years. Distinguished visitors included both King George and Queen Elizabeth II of England, U.S.S.R. foreign minister

V. M. Molotov, and Queen Wilhelmina of the Netherlands. All received a gracious welcome, as did thousands of ordinary citizens who visited with less fanfare.

In 1941 Eleanor assumed her first official government job when she became deputy director of the Office of Civilian Defense under New York's Mayor Fiorello La Guardia. During World War II, she visited American servicemen abroad, which added to the already considerable public esteem and affection in which she was held. She also traveled widely in the United States, regularly giving lectures and radio broadcasts. Partly as a result of Eleanor's outspoken manner and high profile, her political enemies found ground for criticism in her active concern for the national welfare, but "the Flying First Lady" made friends wherever she appeared.

Eleanor first served as a member of the U.S. delegation to the United Nations in 1945, the year her husband died in office and was succeeded by Harry S. Truman. At Truman's behest, she spent six years at the United Nations, to which she returned in 1961, the year before her death. Eventually, after decades of public service, she became known as "the First Lady of the World." Among her publications are *This I Remember* (1949) and her autobiography, published in 1961.

Asked to run for both the Senate and the vice-presidency, Eleanor refused, but she remained a force to be reckoned with in the Democratic Party and in many humanitarian causes. She died in November 1962 and was buried beside her husband at Hyde Park.

Elizabeth Virginia Wallace Truman

1885–1982
30TH FIRST LADY: Apr. 12,
  1945–Jan. 20, 1953
1 Child
"Bess"

D escribed as the "independent woman from Independence," Bess Wallace was born in Missouri, where she
grew up with Harry Truman. They attended local
schools together and were married in May 1919, a month after
Truman returned from his service in World War I.

When Truman was elected to the Senate in 1934, the couple moved
to Washington, D.C., and Bess became Truman's official secretary.
She helped to write speeches and was consulted about his decisions.
Vice-President Truman assumed the presidency when Franklin D.
Roosevelt died in 1945, and Bess immediately ended the press con-
ferences begun by Eleanor Roosevelt. Not comfortable in the spot-
light, she appeared publicly only when necessary. When the White
House was being rebuilt, the Trumans moved across the street into
Blair House, where Bess created miniature versions of the Blue,
Red, and Green Rooms. At her request, the original walls of the
White House were saved for the reconstruction.

The Trumans returned to Independence, Missouri, in 1953.
There they established the Harry S. Truman Library and Truman
wrote his memoirs. Widowed in 1972, Bess remained in
Independence until her death in 1982 and was buried beside her
husband in the courtyard of the Harry S. Truman Library.

Mary Geneva Doud Eisenhower

1896–1979
31ST FIRST LADY: 1953–61

2 Children
"Mamie"

Born in Boone, Iowa, "Mamie" Doud moved with her family to Denver, Colorado, when she was seven. During the winters the Douds traveled to San Antonio, Texas, where, in 1915, Mamie met 2nd Lieutenant Dwight D. Eisenhower. They were married nine months later, in July 1916, and Mamie's years as an army wife began. She estimated that they lived in twenty-seven homes over a thirty-eight year period. General Eisenhower directed Allied war efforts during World War II, while his wife remained in Washington, D.C. In 1948 Eisenhower became president of Columbia University, and the couple purchased their first home, in Gettysburg, Pennsylvania, still under construction when Eisenhower was elected president.

The Eisenhowers entered the White House as a widely loved and respected couple. Mamie resumed the task of sorting and identifying the White House china, which had been neglected for some years. She oversaw all of the planning for state dinners and filled the rooms with fresh flowers, which were then donated to local hospitals. Enjoying her role, she was popular with staff and visitors alike.

Postwar relations resulted in unprecedented numbers of foreign dignitaries and leaders visiting the White House. Mamie's energy was affected by a heart problem and by Ménière's disease, an inner-ear disturbance that caused dizzy spells. However, she continued to play an active role in the Executive Mansion throughout both of her husband's terms. When Eisenhower suffered a heart attack during his second term, the couple reduced their social activities.

After leaving the White House, the Eisenhowers retired to their farm in Gettysburg. In 1969 the Gallup Poll named Mamie the most admired woman in the world. Eisenhower died that same year and Mamie continued to live on the farm until her own death ten years later.

Jacqueline Lee Bouvier Kennedy

1929–94
32ND FIRST LADY: Jan. 20,
1961–Nov. 22, 1963

3 Children
"Jackie"

An independent and cultured woman, Jacqueline Bouvier, known since childhood as Jackie, was one of the most influential and newsworthy First Ladies ever to enter the White House. Born in Southampton, Long Island, to John D. and Janet Lee Bouvier, she was accustomed to a life of privilege from an early age. When her parents divorced in her teens and her mother married Hugh D. Auchincloss, her circumstances remained affluent. She and her sister, the future Lee Radziwill, divided their time between the Auchincloss estate, "Merry Wood," near Washington, D.C., and Newport, Rhode Island. Jackie's early education was at Miss Chapin's School in New York City and Miss Porter's, in Farmington, Connecticut. After spending a year at Vassar College, her studies took her to France, first to Grenoble, then to the Sorbonne in Paris. She completed her college education at George Washington University.

Jackie's experience with public attention began at an early age. A talented horsewoman, she was praised in *The New York Times* for her skill in competitions at Madison Square Garden. In 1947 she was hailed "Debutante of the Year." Her family connections and her own perseverance helped her land the job of "Inquiring Camera Girl" on the Washington *Times-Herald*, a job that would have an impact on her future. She was sent to interview Democratic Senator John F. Kennedy, considered one of the country's most eligible bachelors. They embarked on a two-year courtship that ended in their lavish wedding in Newport in September 1953. Twenty-six bridesmaids and groomsmen attended them, and nine hundred invited guests were present. Crowds almost broke through the police barricades to get a closer look at the elegant bride.

The newlyweds bought a house in McLean, Virginia, where they spent the first few years of their marriage. They then moved to Georgetown, where their daughter Caroline was born in 1957.

Jacqueline Lee Bouvier Kennedy

The political career of "JFK," as he was called, culminated in his 1960 nomination for president. Jackie campaigned with her husband and contributed a column entitled "Campaign Wife" to the Democratic National Committee newspaper. At the time, she was pregnant with John, Jr., who was born shortly before her husband's inauguration in 1961.

Jackie was the third-youngest First Lady in U.S. history, but she showed confidence and maturity beyond her years throughout her time in the role. She was adamant that her children be safeguarded from public scrutiny and immersed herself in the project of restoring the White House. She appointed art directors, museum curators, and historians to advisory committees, resulting in the White House Historical Association, which publishes guidebooks to the Executive Mansion. The profits go to ensuring additional historical purchases for its library and museum. Jackie's televised tour of the newly furnished and restored White House helped garner national support for the project, and donations were generous. To ensure that the gifts would remain in the White House permanently, she sponsored a bill that would declare it an official museum. She also diversified receptions and parties at the Executive Mansion, and replaced unwieldy banquet tables with round tables for small groups.

Edith Head, a Hollywood fashion designer, described Jackie's impact on fashion as "the greatest single influence in history": her sense of style influenced both Americans and Europeans. She also brought the White House to a new level in the realm of cultural events, inviting artists, musicians, and distinguished writers. She was the first president's wife to have her own press secretary.

Fluent in French and Spanish, Jackie made an important contribution to her husband's missions abroad. Always socially adept, she charmed foreign leaders with her knowledge about art; beauty, intelligence, and style were additional assets. In 1963 she gave birth to a premature son, Patrick, who died just a few days later. Before Caroline's birth, she had suffered a miscarriage and delivered a stillborn daughter. Her surviving son and daughter, the first young children of a president in fifty years, were treasured all the more by both parents after these experiences.

Jackie accompanied JFK on the ill-fated trip to Dallas, Texas, in November 1963. As they passed through the city in a convertible car, JFK was shot by an assassin. His stunned wife held him in her arms, shielded by a Secret Service agent, as the car was driven to Parkland Memorial Hospital, where the president was declared dead on arrival.

Lyndon Johnson was sworn in as president only an hour and a half after the tragedy; Jackie was at his side still wearing her blood-stained clothing. The nation mourned with the poised widow, whose dignity throughout the state funeral won her millions of admirers. With the president's brothers, she walked behind his coffin to Arlington National Cemetery, where she lighted an eternal flame at his grave.

Before leaving the White House, Jackie erected a memorial plaque to JFK in the presidential bedroom. She and her two children moved first to Georgetown, then to New York City, where she hoped to lead a private life away from the attention of the media. However, public interest in her remained high throughout her second marriage, to wealthy Greek shipping magnate Aristotle Onassis, who died in 1975. Jackie returned to New York City, where she bought a large cooperative apartment on Fifth Avenue. She worked as an editor at Doubleday until her death in 1994 and was buried at Arlington National Cemetery near the grave of John F. Kennedy.

Claudia Alta Taylor Johnson

b. 1912

33RD FIRST LADY: Nov. 22,
1963–Jan. 20, 1969

2 Children

"Lady Bird"

Claudia Taylor, of Karnack, Texas, was called "Lady Bird" from an early age — an appropriate nickname for the woman who would show such concern for conservation. She graduated from the University of Texas with degrees in journalism and liberal arts and in 1934 met Lyndon Baines Johnson, a Congressional secretary, whom she married two months later.

Lady Bird was dedicated to her husband's career and financed his congressional campaign. A good businesswoman, she transformed a thirty-thousand-dollar investment in a radio and television station into a five-million-dollar enterprise. Nicknamed "LBJ," her husband became Senate majority leader and was elected JFK's vice-president in 1960. Lady Bird assumed many responsibilities and traveled to thirty-three countries as a goodwill ambassador. When the president was assassinated in 1963, her husband succeeded him and Lady Bird launched her own agenda.

Declaring that she wanted to "boast about America," she created The First Lady's Committee for a More Beautiful Capital, an organization whose scope soon expanded to include the entire nation. She joined her husband in the War on Poverty, visiting ghettoes and tirelessly supporting the Head Start program for underprivileged children.

Johnson chose not to run for re-election in 1968, and the couple retired to their LBJ Ranch in Texas. Before Johnson's death in 1973, they worked together on the Lyndon Baines Johnson Library, and Lady Bird published her *White House Diary* (1971). In 1981 *The First Lady, A Portrait of Lady Bird Johnson*, a documentary film about her contribution to her husband's years as president was released. Today, Lady Bird serves on the Board of the National Geographic Society as a trustee emeritus and supports the National Wildflower Research Center, an organization that she founded in 1982. She remains devoted to her husband's memory, her children, and her grandchildren.

Thelma Catherine Ryan Nixon

1912–1993
34TH FIRST LADY: Jan. 20,
   1969–Aug. 9, 1974
2 Children
"Pat"

Because she was born on the eve of St. Patrick's Day in 1912, Thelma Ryan was nicknamed Pat. The family moved from Nevada to California, where her mother died, leaving thirteen-year-old Pat with the care of her father and two brothers. Her father died when she was seventeen, and she completed her high school education a few months later. She graduated with honors from the University of Southern California in 1937.

After college Pat accepted a teaching job in Whittier, where she met Richard Nixon, a recent graduate of the Law School at Duke University. They were married in June 1940 and moved to Washington, D.C., where Pat gave birth to two daughters. Nixon was elected to the presidency in 1968 and won again easily in 1972. As First Lady Pat dedicated herself to continuing Lady Bird Johnson's "Beautification" program and she organized "hands-on" tours for the blind. She traveled more than any of her predecessors, fostering good will and encouraging volunteer work.

Nixon was forced to resign as president in 1974 after the Watergate scandal. Pat stood by her husband — the first president to resign the office — despite the controversy surrounding him, earning the respect of the American public. She died on June 22, 1993, just ten months before her husband.

Elizabeth Anne Bloomer Warren Ford

b. 1918
35TH FIRST LADY: Aug. 9,
  1974–Jan. 20, 1977
4 Children
"Betty"

B etty Bloomer was a keen dancer who worked with the Martha Graham troupe in New York City, supporting herself as a fashion model. She returned to her home town, Grand Rapids, Michigan, to become fashion coordinator for a department store, teaching dance to handicapped children in her spare time. Her marriage to William Warren when she was twenty-four ended in divorce four years later.

Betty married Gerald R. Ford during his successful 1948 congressional campaign and over the next ten years gave birth to four children. When Ford ascended to the presidency after Nixon's resignation, Betty declared that "the White House has been like a grave…I want it to sing." A forthright woman, Betty candidly discussed her battle with breast cancer to raise public awareness of the disease. She also actively supported the Equal Rights Amendment. The Fords did much to reassure the American public after the Watergate scandal.

In retirement in California, Betty continues to champion the rights of women and share her love of dance. She was instrumental in establishing the Betty Ford Center for treatment of alcohol and drug dependency, having frankly acknowledged her own successful struggle with addiction.

Rosalynn Smith Carter

b. 1927
36TH FIRST LADY: 1977–1981
4 Children

Rosalynn Smith and Jimmy Carter were neighbors in their native Plains, Georgia, and Carter had announced his desire to marry Rosalynn when she was only seventeen and he twenty years old. On July 7, 1946, that plan was fulfilled. Carter served in the Navy for seven years until his father's death in 1953, when he resigned to take over the family's peanut farming business. Rosalynn's assumption of these responsibilities allowed Carter to enter politics in 1962.

Rosalynn has described her relationship with Carter as "more a political partner than a political wife," and she was an important part of his campaign team, bringing her experience with her to the White House. Partly as a result of her acumen, Carter narrowly defeated Gerald Ford in the 1976 presidential election.

As First Lady, Rosalynn attended Cabinet meetings and often represented her husband at ceremonial occasions. Officially, she served as the president's personal emissary to Latin American countries. She was an outspoken supporter of women's rights, and her interest in mental health programs enabled her to serve as Honorary Chairperson of the President's Commission on Mental Health (1977–78).

Carter's presidency was marked by economic problems, including burgeoning inflation. Despite his success in securing the Camp David peace agreement between Israel and Egypt, and other achievements, he lost the 1980 election to Ronald Reagan by a wide margin. Since leaving the White House, the couple have maintained their strong commitment to public service.

Honored in 1980 for her "commitment…to build a more caring society," Rosalynn serves as a director of the Carter Center, where she continues her interest in mental health and human-rights issues and volunteers with Habitat for Humanity. Her autobiography, *First Lady From Plains* (1984), tells the story of her years in the White House.

Anne Frances Robbins Davis Reagan

b. 1923

37TH FIRST LADY: 1981−1989

2 Children

"Nancy"

Nancy Davis was born Anne Frances Robbins on July 6, 1932, in New York City. Her mother, a stage actress, married Dr. Loyal Davis, a neurosurgeon, in 1938. After graduating from Smith College in Massachusetts as a theater major, Nancy moved back to New York City, where she became a professional actress, performing in eleven films between 1949 and 1956. Her acting career ended with the movie *Hellcats of the Navy*, in which she starred with Ronald Reagan.

Nancy had met Reagan in 1951 when he was president of the Screen Actors Guild, and the two were married a year later. Nancy devoted herself to her husband and two children, abandoning her career as an actress. As Reagan's political career progressed, his wife gave increasing time and energy to charitable organizations for emotionally and physically handicapped and the elderly. When she became First Lady in 1981, she used her influence to bring national attention to such concerns by sponsoring groups like the Foster Grandparent Program.

After Reagan was injured by an assassination attempt just two months after his first inauguration, Nancy continued to raise public awareness of social problems. Her commitment to keeping children off drugs was expressed in the slogan "Just Say No." She visited prevention and rehabilitation centers to encourage youngsters to stay free of drugs. To demonstrate the ability of talented young performers, she organized concerts at the White House that were broadcast on the PBS television special "In Performance at the White House." She also renovated the second and third floors of the mansion.

In 1989 Nancy published *My Turn*, a book about her years as First Lady. Nancy's commitment to her husband, diagnosed with Alzheimer's Disease in 1994, remains steadfast. She was by his side when Maureen, Reagan's eldest child from his first marriage, died of cancer on August 8, 2001, at the age of 60.

Barbara Pierce Bush

b. 1925
38TH FIRST LADY: 1989−93
6 Children

Admired by the American public for her common-sense attitude, capability, and sincerity, Barbara Pierce was born in Rye, New York, on June 8, 1925, and attended public and private schools, including Rye Country Day School, Ashley Hall, in South Carolina, and Smith College. Barbara and George Bush met in 1941, but did not marry until January 6, 1945, after Bush had returned from his service as a Navy pilot in World War II.

Barbara became accustomed to life as a high-profile political wife during her husband's years in the House of Representatives (from 1966), as director of the Central Intelligence Agency (from 1976), and as vice-president (from 1981). No other First Lady had entered the White House with such extensive experience.

When Bush became president in 1989, Barbara brought national attention to the problem of illiteracy, organizing the Barbara Bush Foundation for Family Literacy. She continued Nancy Reagan's initiative against drugs and raised public awareness of AIDS. Her example of volunteerism was a major contribution.

In 1993 the Bushes retired to their home in Houston, Texas, where Barbara continues her humanitarian work. She continues to encourage volunteer work, declaring that "If it worries you, then you've got to do something about it."

Hillary Diane Rodham Clinton

b. 1947
39TH FIRST LADY: 1993—2001
1 Child

Hillary Rodham was the eldest child of Hugh and Dorothy Rodham. She grew up in Park Ridge, Illinois, with her two brothers and entered Wellesley College in 1965. An excellent student, she graduated with honors and attended Yale University's School of Law, where she met fellow student Bill Clinton.

After she left Yale, Hillary became a staff attorney for the Children's Defense Fund. A year later, in 1974, the Impeachment Inquiry staff of the Judiciary Committee of the House of Representatives recruited her to work with them. She left Washington, D.C., for Arkansas after her 1975 marriage to Clinton. However, she retained her maiden name until 1982. During the early years of their marriage, both the Clintons joined the faculty of law at the University of Arkansas in Fayetteville.

Hillary's concern for children deepened with the birth of her daughter, Chelsea, in 1980. She founded the Arkansas Advocates for Children and Families and served on the board of the Arkansas Children's Hospital. Energetic and determined, she demonstrated a strong commitment to improving educational standards and access: she became chairwoman of the Arkansas Education Standards Committee and created the Home Instruction Program for Preschool Youngsters, which helped underprivileged families prepare their children for school. By 1984 Hillary had received several state honors: Arkansas' Woman of the Year (1983) and Young Mother of the Year (1984).

Hillary brought twelve years of experience as a governor's wife to the White House when Clinton won the presidential election of 1992. An advocate of women's rights, she provided her husband with a list of candidates for a variety of high-level positions. Donna Shalala was appointed secretary of health and human services, and Janet Reno became attorney general. Hillary herself was appointed head of Clinton's task force on Health Care Reform. Breaking precedent, she set up her office in the West Wing of the White House with the rest of the presidential staff, rather than in the East Wing.

During trips to Asia in 1995 and at the United Nations, she called for new opportunities for women around the world. An able public speaker, she has made women's and children's rights a high priority. She has contributed to White House history by restoring the Treaty Room and the Lincoln Sitting Room to their former Victorian splendor. Her book *It Takes a Village* testifies to her commitment to children's welfare, and she has urged fellow citizens to "reach across the lines that divide us, not with pointing fingers but with outstretched hands."

On November 8, 2000, Hillary Clinton was elected by a 55 to 43 percent margin over Congressman Rick Lazio, becoming the first woman senator from New York State and the only first lady to win public office. She was sworn into office on January 3, 2001.

On the 6-month anniversary of the September 11, 2001, terrorist attacks, Hillary addressed students at Harvard University, declaring: "Out of the crucible of death and destruction we can forge a stronger, safer world."

Laura Welch Bush

b. 1946
40TH FIRST LADY: 2001–Present
2 Children

L aura Welch was born an only child in Midland, Texas, to Harold B. Welch, a successful home builder, and Jenna Welch, who worked as her husband's bookkeeper. A dedicated student, Laura attended Southern Methodist University in Dallas, where she received a degree in education. She went on to earn her master's degree in library science from the University of Texas in 1973.

After graduating, Laura moved to Austin, where she worked as an elementary school teacher and librarian for a decade before meeting George W. Bush. After a three-month courtship, George and Laura were married in November 1977. In 1981 Laura gave birth to fraternal twin daughters, Barbara and Jenna, who are named for their grandmothers.

An advocate of children's rights and education, Laura's career as first lady began officially on January 16, 2001, when George W. Bush became the second president to hold office after his father, George H. W. Bush.

During a radio address to the Nation on November 17, 2001, which exposed the horrors of the Taliban regime, Laura Bush declared that "the fight against terrorism is also a fight for the rights and dignity of women."

Acknowledgments

All photographs are courtesy of the Library of Congress, Prints and Photographs Division, except those supplied by the following individuals and institutions, to whom grateful acknowledgment is made for permission to reproduce photographs: Bush Presidential Library p.60; Corbis-Bettmann p.18, 21, 23, 29, 30, 33, 34, 36, 38, 40, 62; Dwight D. Eisenhower Library (portrait by Thomas E. Stephens) p.46; Gerald R. Ford Library p.55; Harry S. Truman Library (by Greta Kempton) p.45; Herbert Hoover Presidential Library-Museum p.41; Independence National Historical Park p.8, 12; James K. Polk Memorial Association p.20; Jimmy Carter Library p.56; © Mark Shaw/Photo Researchers p.48; LBJ Library Collection (portrait by Robert Knudsen) p.52; National Park Service/Adams National Historic Site p.10, 15; National Park Service/Andrew Johnson National Historic Site p.26; Nixon Presidential Materials/National Archives and Records Administration p.54; President Benjamin Harrison Home p.17; Ronald Reagan Library p.58; Copyrighted by the White House Historical Association p.14 (Courtesy of Thomas J. and William K. Edwards), 42; Courtesy of the White House, Press Office of Hillary Clinton, p.62; The White House (Official White House Photograph by Eric Draper) p.63.